GETTING TO KNOW
THE U.S. PRESIDENTS

G E O R G E
WASHINGTON

FIRST PRESIDENT
1789 – 1797

WRITTEN AND ILLUSTRATED BY MIKE VENEZIA

CHILDREN'S PRESS®
A DIVISION OF SCHOLASTIC INC.
NEW YORK   TORONTO   LONDON   AUCKLAND   SYDNEY
MEXICO CITY   NEW DELHI   HONG KONG
DANBURY, CONNECTICUT

For my First Lady, Jeannine

Reading Consultant: Nanci R. Vargus, Ed.D., Assistant Professor, School of Education, University of Indianapolis

Historical Consultant: Marc J. Selverstone, Ph.D., Assistant Professor, Miller Center of Public Affairs, University of Virginia

Photographs © 2004:
Art Resource, NY: 3, 26 (Reunion des Musees Nationaux/Gerard Blot), 17 (Reunion des Musees Nationaux/El Meliani)
Metropolitan Museum of Art: 31 (Gift of Edgar William and Bernice Chrysler Garbisch, 1963. (63.201.2), photograph © 1983, *Washington Reviewing the Western Army at Fort Cumberland, Maryland,* by Frederick Kemmelmeyer, oil on canvas, 22 3/4 in. x 37 1/4 in.), 22 (Gift of John Stewart Kennedy, 1897. (97.34), photograph © 1992, *Washington Crossing the Delaware,* by Emanuel Gottlieb Leutze, oil on canvas, 149 x 255 in.)
National Gallery of Art, Washington, D.C.: 10 (Gift of Edgar William and Bernice Chrysler Garbisch, Image © 2003 Board of Trustees, *The End of the Hunt,* by American 19th Century, 1800, oil on canvas, 34 1/2 x 53 7/8)
Stock Montage, Inc.: 24
Superstock, Inc.: 32 (Blerancourt, Chateau/Lauros-Giraudon, Paris), 4, 19, 29
Washington and Lee University, Lexington, Va./Washington-Custis Lee Collection: 16 right, 16 left

Colorist for illustrations: Dave Ludwig

Library of Congress Cataloging-in-Publication Data

Venezia, Mike.
  George Washington / written and illustrated by Mike Venezia.
     p. cm. — (Getting to know the U.S. presidents)
Summary: An introduction to the life of George Washington, a brave man and good military leader who became the nation's first president.
  ISBN 0-516-22606-1 (lib. bdg.)   0-516-27475-9 (pbk.)
  1. Washington, George, 1732-1799—Juvenile literature. 2.
Presidents—United States—Biography—Juvenile literature. [1.
Washington, George, 1732-1799. 2. Presidents.] I. Title.
  E312.66.V46 2004
  973.4'1'092–dc21

                              2003000015

3 4 5 6 7 8 9 10 R 13 12 11 10 09 08 07

A portrait of George Washington after the 1777 Battle of Princeton, by Charles Willson Peale

George Washington was the first president of the United States of America. He was born in Westmoreland County, Virginia, in 1732. He died in Mount Vernon, Virginia, in 1799.

A portrait of George Washington by Gilbert Stuart

A lot of pictures of George Washington make him look kind of serious or grumpy. That's because his teeth weren't in very good shape. He held his mouth closed tightly so nobody had to look at them.

He also wore a wig, which makes him look a little unusual to us, but back then it was the style. Everyone was wearing them.

Actually, George Washington was pretty friendly. On certain days he invited anyone who was passing by his house to stop in and chat—as long as they dressed nicely.

He also loved parties and barbecues.
He liked to dance, and he liked to tell jokes.

George Washington was born on his father's tobacco farm in Virginia. His father had lots of land. The Washingtons were pretty wealthy.

Virginia was one of the thirteen colonies that made up what would become the United States of America. The colonies were owned by England and ruled by the king of England. Everyone born in the colonies was an English citizen, including George Washington.

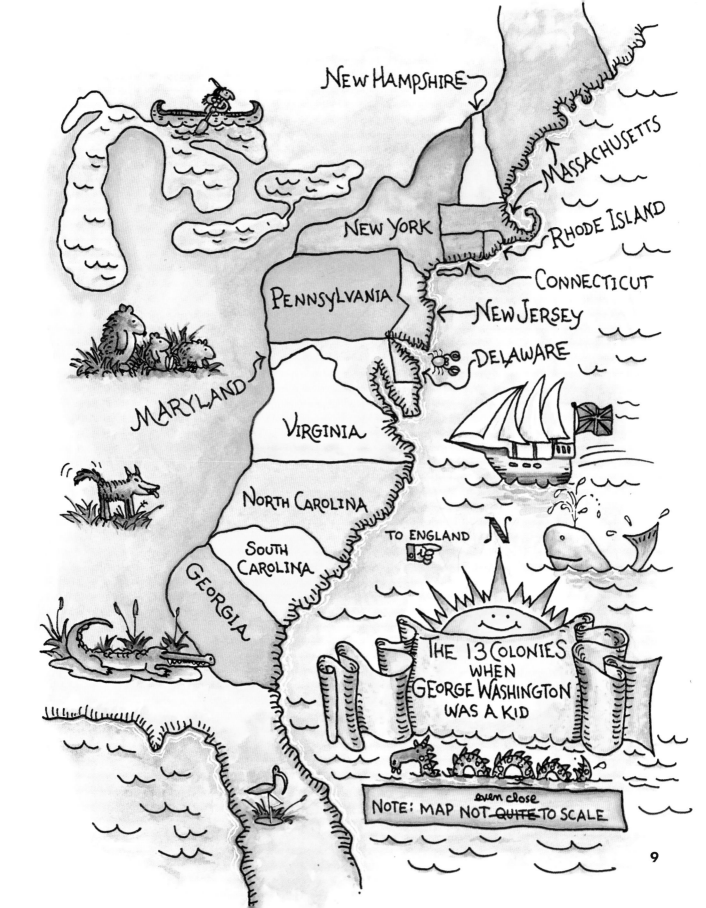

NEW HAMPSHIRE

MASSACHUSETTS

RHODE ISLAND

NEW YORK

CONNECTICUT

NEW JERSEY

PENNSYLVANIA

DELAWARE

MARYLAND

VIRGINIA

NORTH CAROLINA

SOUTH CAROLINA

GEORGIA

TO ENGLAND

N

THE 13 COLONIES
WHEN
GEORGE WASHINGTON
WAS A KID

NOTE: MAP NOT ~~QUITE~~ even close TO SCALE

The End of the Hunt, a painting showing a hunting party in Virginia, unknown artist (National Gallery of Art, Washington, D.C.)

When George was very young, he learned to ride a horse and hunt. There were lots of places for him to explore. In the 1700s, Virginia was mainly forests and wilderness.

George was a good student in school. When he was sixteen, he decided to become a surveyor. A surveyor measures land and makes maps for landowners so they know exactly what they own. People paid George quite a lot of money for doing this.

George spent a lot of time surveying outdoors in the wilderness. He learned things that would later help him to become a great leader. He slept outdoors, hunted, and got to know the American Indians who lived there. It must have been quite a change from his life back home.

When George Washington was twenty-one, he decided he would like to be a soldier in Virginia's army. Even though George didn't know anything about being a soldier, the governor of Virginia gave him a chance.

This was the beginning of a great career for George Washington.

During this time, French people and American Indians were starting to build forts in the Ohio Valley. The English became angry. They felt that the land in the Ohio Valley belonged to them. Someone had to go tell the French to leave. The only one brave enough to volunteer was George Washington.

The governor of Virginia sent George
on this dangerous mission, but things didn't
work out very well.

When the governor found out what had happened, he sent George back to the Ohio Valley with a whole bunch of soldiers to try again. On the way, George ran into some French soldiers camping and had a battle with them. This turned out to be the beginning of the French and Indian War.

The French and Indian War took a long time to straighten out, but finally the English won. George Washington was able to show what a good leader he was.

Portraits of Martha Dandridge Custis (left) and her children, John and Martha Parke Custis (right), by John Wollaston (Washington and Lee University, Lexington, Virginia)

After the war, George went back to Virginia to take care of his family's farm. He was elected to help run Virginia, and married a woman named Martha Custis. Martha already had two children from an earlier marriage. George had plenty of things to keep him busy.

By the late 1700s, people in the colonies were getting pretty fed up with the way the king of England was running things. He told all the colonists to give him lots of money. This was known as taxation. He told the colonists they had to take English soldiers into their houses, feed them, and give them a place to sleep. He told people they could buy only things that came from England. He did a lot of things that weren't very nice.

A portrait of King George III of England (Chateaux de Versailles et deTrianon, Versailles)

The king of England and the English government had been treating the colonists badly for a long time. Finally, in 1775, people became so angry they decided to do something about it. The men and women of the thirteen colonies started fighting the English. They wanted their freedom. This was the beginning of the Revolutionary War.

George Washington was asked if he would head up the colonies' army. People knew George was brave and a good leader.

George, too, was angry about the way the English were treating the colonists. So, on June 15, 1775, George Washington agreed to become the commander of all the soldiers in the thirteen colonies.

A painting by Eugene Hess showing George Washington commanding the colonial army (Maximelaneum Foundation, Munich, Germany)

Heading up a new army was very difficult. Many colonists wanted to help fight the English, but most of these people knew nothing about being a soldier. General Washington worked hard with the men he found and was able to turn them into pretty good soldiers.

The Revolutionary War lasted about eight years. Most of the time, the powerful British army seemed to be winning. At a certain point, after losing a few battles, General Washington knew he would have to win one pretty soon or his men might give up. He decided to take a chance. On Christmas Day in 1776, he gathered his men onto boats, crossed the icy Delaware River, and headed for the town of Trenton, New Jersey.

George Washington Crossing the Delaware, by Emanuel Leutze
(The Metropolitan Museum of Art, New York)

Trenton was being guarded by about a thousand Hessian soldiers. Hessian soldiers were German soldiers hired by England to help fight the colonists. The Hessians were completely surprised and gave up right away. They didn't expect anyone to attack them on Christmas!

General Washington and his men at Valley Forge, Pennsylvania, during the terrible winter of 1777-78

In 1777, General Washington and his army spent the whole winter with hardly any food or shelter. It was one of the wettest, snowiest, and coldest winters ever at Valley Forge. Some of the soldiers didn't even have shoes or boots.

General Washington and his soldiers never gave up, though, and when that winter was over, only the strongest and most loyal men were left. General Washington's army was now better than ever.

The colonial army kept improving. Then something happened that really helped them out. The country of France decided to help General Washington fight the English. The French didn't like England very much during that time and wanted the colonists to win the war. In October 1781, with the help of French soldiers and warships, George Washington and his army trapped the British army in Yorktown, Virginia, and made them give up.

The British surrendering to General Washington at Yorktown, Virginia, in 1781

The war was over, and the United States of America was officially a new country! George Washington was ready to go home to Martha and take some time off to relax.

At least he thought he was going to take some time off to relax. It seems the American people had something else in mind for him to do.

The United States needed a leader—someone who could help get things off to a good start. They needed someone who was brave, smart, and well liked. Most importantly, they needed a leader they could trust. The American people wanted George Washington to be their first president. Not only was he the best man for the job, but George looked like a good leader. He was 6 feet, 2 inches tall, and handsome.

One reason people trusted George Washington so much was that he had done something quite remarkable. George Washington had turned down the chance to be a king. After the Revolutionary War ended, some of Washington's closest friends tried to convince him to be king of the United States!

George Washington hated that idea. He had just fought a long, hard war to free the colonies from the rule of King George III. Washington thought the leader of the United States should be elected by the people and be in charge for only a limited time. *That* type of leader George was willing to be.

George Washington taking the presidential oath of office on April 30, 1789

In 1789, George Washington was elected the first president of the United States of America. He promised to protect the rights of the American people. He also promised to follow the rules of the U.S. Constitution, which was kind of a guide written to help start up the new country.

As the first president, George Washington worked hard to set things up. He helped organize a place to make money called a mint. He then helped start up banks and the U.S. Post Office.

George Washington was really surprised to see that some of his advisors and other members of the government began to argue and disagree a lot. Many of them had different ideas about how to run the new country. President Washington tried as hard as he could to convince everyone to work together to keep the new government from falling apart.

A painting attributed to Frederick Kemmelmeyer showing President Washington viewing the army he called in to put down the Whiskey Rebellion (The Metropolitan Museum of Art, New York)

Once, when a bunch of angry farmers refused to pay taxes on the whiskey they made, George Washington sent U.S. soldiers to convince them to change their minds. This event was called the Whiskey Rebellion. It was an important test that showed that the new government had the power to enforce its laws.

A portrait of George Washington by Samuel King (Chateau Blerancourt, Paris)

George Washington was one of the greatest Americans ever. He was a brave general. Without him, the thirteen colonies might not have won their freedom from England. He worked very hard as the first president to make sure the United States got off to a good start. That's why George Washington is called the Father of His Country.